Jake is a Magic Carpet Pilot

Jake Stories Publishing

www.jakestories.com

Illustration by Jake Stories Publishing

Children's stories and Jake Brain Training Games

Story by Charles J LaBelle

Jake Stories Publishing
Children's Stories and Jake Brain Training Games

www.jakestories.com
© 2015 Charles J. LaBelle

National Library Archives of Canada
LaBelle, Charles J.
Jake is a Magic Carpet Pilot Revised Edition 2016
Illustration by Jake Stories Publishing
ISBN 978-1-896710-50-1

Chapter One
They Came From Outer Space

The fall weekend was cool and wet.
Mist cast ghostly shadows on empty streets.

Even the robins were tucked in their nests.

Only the crows were out, frantically calling;

Caw, caw, caw.

Whoosh ! A sudden gust of damp wind chilled Jake.
He pulled his sweater tight around his neck and sang,
♫*Piff piff, boom boom, I wish it was June.*
Little shivers can be fun but I prefer the warm, warm sun.
I wait on the veranda for Aunt Joan and Uncle Jack,
and my favorite cousins Zoe and Zac.
I'm glad they're coming; it's damp and cold.
It makes me sniffle and sneeze.
The wind blows through my pants and gives me goosebumps on my knees. ♫

Jake stopped singing and thought about his aunt and uncle.
He remembered the story Gram told him . . .
"People in Tillerville are not sure about Uncle Jack and Aunt Joan.
They think they're strange looking people from another planet.
Your aunt and uncle do look different. They have long pointed ears.
When they get excited, the hair on their ears stands straight up.

Their history is also very unusual.
They appeared out of nowhere on the same day that a UFO was reported over our town. People in Tillerville saw two meteors streak through the night sky. That night, crowds searched for the meteors. Instead, they found two disks, one gold and one silver. Each disk had a beautiful baby tucked inside. They landed beside the orphanage steps. The next morning, the police found two spaceship heat shields nearby in a farmer's field.

A note was attached to the inside of the gold disk:
**'These two children, Joan and Jack, are not brother and sister,
but they must remain together all their lives.'**

I adopted Uncle Jack and Aunt Joan.
I raised them with my son, who is your dad.

When the children grew up they got married.
Your Dad was best man at their wedding.
And that's why you have an aunt and uncle
and two cousins with pointy ears."

Chapter Two
Uncle Jack's Invention

Jake thought, *Today is a special day; it's Zac's birthday.*
Uncle Jack always plans a fun surprise. I wonder what it will be this year?

My cousins don't look alike except for their ears.
Zac has big round brown eyes.
His curly brown hair covers most of his ears.
This is a good thing because his big ears come to a point.
They have long black hair along the edges.
He looks just like Uncle Jack.

Zoe is different.
She has big green eyes, carrot red hair, and a very pretty button nose.
She has lovely pointed ears that poke through her hair.
She looks just like Aunt Joan.

Jake shouted, "Here they come!"
Suddenly a car flashed through the mist.
It was lit up like a Christmas tree.

Uncle Jack said, "The more lights you have on your car
the less chance of someone hitting you."

He shouted to Jake as he pulled up to the front door,
"Hooray! We're going for a picnic in the rain!
It's cool! We'll have the picnic grounds all to ourselves."

Jake opened the car door and settled into the big fluffy seat in the
back/front of the car.

He said, "Wow! I knew it was you Uncle Jack!
I could see all your blinking lights."

Uncle Jack backed out of the driveway.
He continued to back down the street.

Jake looked amazed and asked,
"This is a different way to drive. Is this another invention?"

Uncle Jack said, "Yes it is.
You never know when you might have to go the other way fast.
When I drive backwards I use my computer WI-FI atomic radar.
And I have two sets of headlights, one set on the front,
and one set on the back."

Rain began to pour. Uncle Jack said," It might be too wet for a picnic."

Jake, Zac and Zoe cried, "Oh, no!"
They huddled in the car, cold and disappointed.
Suddenly a huge bolt of lightning flashed across the sky.
The thunder came immediately.

Jake said, "We're in the middle of a big bad storm. I have never seen so much lightning. Look! There's more. It must be close.

I bet you can't say, *'Dogs and cats and one,'* before the thunder booms."

Boom !

They couldn't say, *Dogs and cats and one,* before the thunder boomed.

Jake said, "This is wild! The lightning must be very close.
I have a feeling something wonderful will happen."

Uncle Jack shouted over the thunder,
"Let's go to the flea market. Let's get out of the rain!
Let's find some treasure!"

Zac whispered to Zoe and Jake, "The hairs on my ears are standing up.
You're right, Jake! Something wonderful is going to happen."

Zoe whispered, "What will it be?"

Zac whispered back, "I don't know but it will be something really big."
The wind howled. Dark, scary faces jumped out of the clouds.
The lightning flashed. The thunder boomed. It was a very strange day.

Chapter Three

Jake's Prediction Comes True

Other cars pulled off to the side with their flashers on.
Jake's uncle just kept driving backwards.
All the lights and the radar screen mounted on the steering wheel made driving easy for Uncle Jack.

He said, "My inventions will change the world someday."

Jake cheered, "Hooray! I know they will Uncle Jack."
Jake had taught Mr. Tiller's 'Silly-Songs' to the twins.
Everyone sang.

♪♪*If you eat a worm, it's not too good for you.*
It will tickle in your throat and end up in your shoe.
Ho! Ho! Ho!
They wiggle and they squiggle from your top to bottom quick.
The only way you get them out is chase them with a stick.
Tickle, tickle, tickle!
from your head down to your toes.
If the worms get inside you, they will eat off all your toes.♪♪

Finally they arrived at the flea market and dashed for the door.

woosh !

A force like a big hand lifted them into the air.

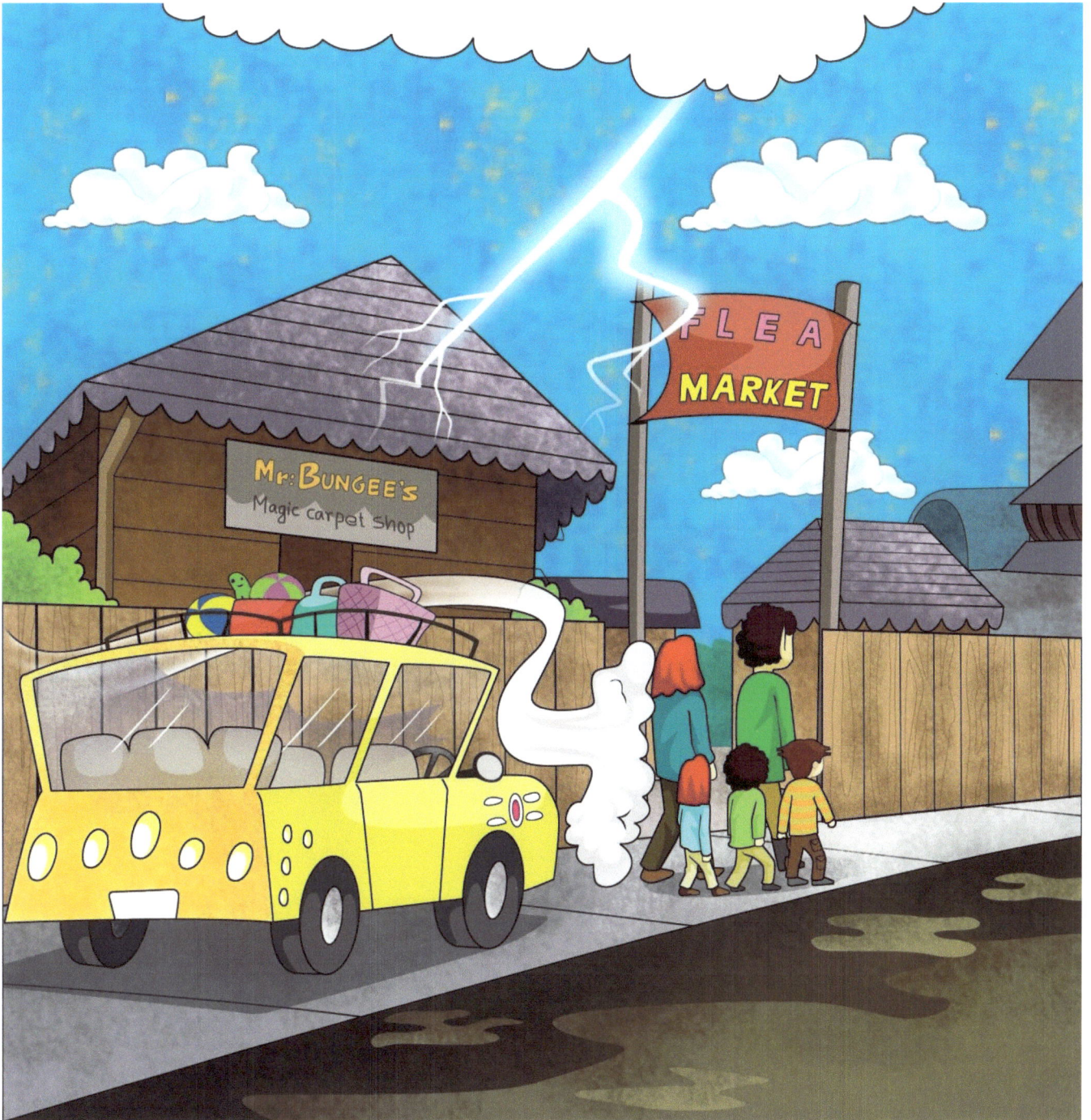

It lifted and pushed them right into the entrance.

Aunt Joan asked,
"Is everyone alright?"

She turned to count them just to make sure.

KABOOM ! crashed the thunder.

FLASH ! streaked the lightning.

A smoking hole appeared in the parking lot where they had stood
seconds before.

sizzle ... *sizzle*

Fire raced across the pavement and died.

Jake cried, "Wow! I knew this was going to be a special day."

Zac shouted,
"The hair on my pointed ears is standing straight up
like the bristles on Zoe's hairbrush!"

As they turned to look inside the flea market
they couldn't believe their eyes.

There, in front of them, floated a beautiful carpet.

The carpet's bright red edges had intricate designs of magical dancing
animals and flowers all around it.

Stars shone from other parts of the carpet.
The outside glowed with a yellow light.

The center of the carpet was the most interesting.
It showed a mixed blue, green and gray sky full of lightning and clouds
with scary faces.

Jake said,
"Piff piff, boom boom, the scary faces in the carpet look the same as the
scary faces in the clouds in the storm."

Uncle Jack answered,
"That's strange. I wonder why?"

Chapter Four

The Ride !

A small shop on their left had a big sign over the door:
We Sell

Magic Carpets

Two people stood Next to the sign.

They looked like Jake's aunt and uncle. They had pointed hairy ears.
"Hello. I'm Mr. Peterson," said Uncle Jack as he extended his hand.

"I'm Mr. Bungee and I'm glad to meet you," said the man.
He looked like Uncle Jack's twin.

All the while, he bobbed up and down as though he was attached to an elastic rope. It made Jake dizzy.

Boing ! Boing ! Boing !

"I'm Mrs. Bungee," said the lady. She looked like Aunt Joan's twin sister.
All the time she talked, she bobbed up and down.

Mr. Bungee wore a red hat and Mrs. Bungee wore a green hat.

"Are we related?" asked Uncle Jack.

"Only if you're from St. Joseph's Orphanage," said Mr. Bungee.

Uncle Jack answered, "Yes, I am and so is my wife. We were found there after the UFO was spotted over Tillerville."

WE SELL
MAGIC CARPETS

Mr. Bungee said, "That's extraordinary! Our story is exactly the same. We must be related somehow. This is wonderful. This is meant to be."

Boing! Boing! Boing!

Mr. Bungee kept bouncing and said, "Have we got the carpet for you. Yes, this flying one is meant just for you. Try it out. I'm sure you're the ones."

Uncle Jack asked, "What do you mean, try it out?" His head bobbed up and down while trying to look Mr. Bungee square in the eye.

Boing! Boing! Boing!

The bouncing Mrs. Bungee said, "You and your family hop on and go for a ride."

Uncle Jack asked, "It's Zac's birthday! Can he steer it? Can we all get on?"

"I don't see why not," said Mr. Bungee.

Zac and Jake climbed on the front of the beautiful carpet. It was still floating three feet off the ground.

Everyone else climbed on. Jake said, "I knew this was going to be a special day."

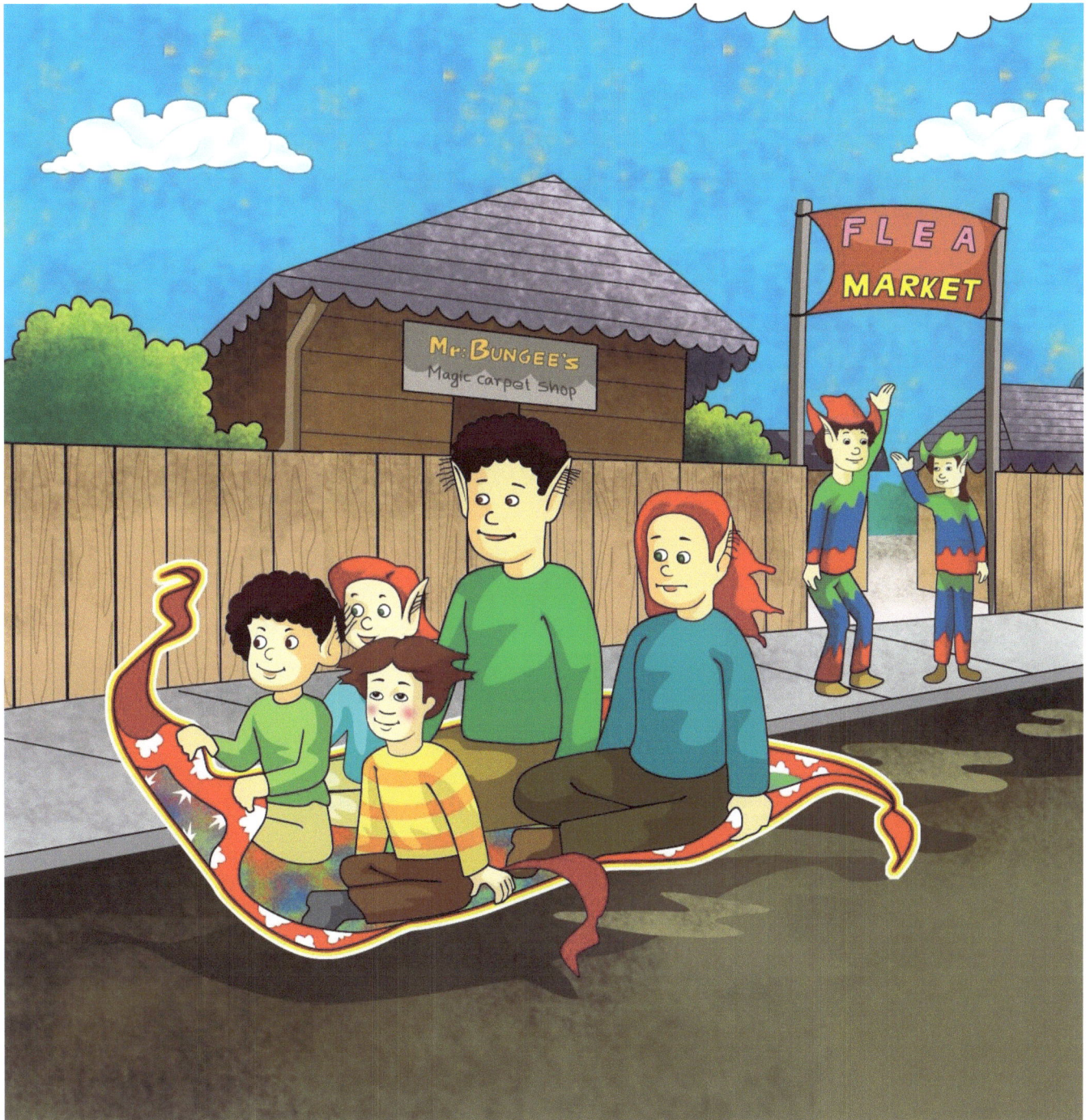

"This is amazing! How do you steer it?" shouted Zac.

Mr. Bungee replied,
"The person at the front controls the carpet.
Just think of where you want to go and say slow or fast."

Zac thought about a *trip out the door*. He shouted, **Fast !**

Mr. Bungee opened the door just in time.
Out they went, all five of them sitting on a flying carpet.

The clouds were gone, the sun appeared, and the carpet skimmed along about three feet above the sidewalk.

Uncle Jack shouted, "Wow! We have to buy this carpet!"

Zac shouted above the wind,
"Can we go just a little further and wave to our friends?"

Uncle Jack replied, "Be quick, Zac, we don't want to lose our chance to buy this wonderful carpet."

"Okay Dad," shouted Zac. "It will be a short, fast trip."

Zac shouted **Extra fast !** He thought of his friends playing in the park.
The carpet zoomed faster and faster!

Whoosh !

Chapter Five

Jake is a Carpet Pilot

Jake could feel his face going flat and his eyes getting big.

The black hairs on Uncle Jack's ears stood up as stiff and straight as Aunt Joan's hair brush.

Zac looked scared. He shouted, **"Slow down!"**
but the carpet went faster.
Zac screamed "**Oh no! What do I do now?**"

Jake pulled himself closer to the front and took control.
He grabbed the carpet's edge and thought,

Slow down !

He whispered, **"Slow down !"**

Then he thought about returning to Mr. Bungee's store.
They returned to the store with Jake piloting all the way back.

After that exciting ride everyone got off.
They wanted to use the washroom . . . except Jake.

He forgot about the washroom. He wanted to be a carpet pilot.

Jake said, **" Slow ! "**

The carpet moved around the store with ease.

He thought of places in the store he wanted to go.

The carpet went there.
It was like a dream.

Things changed quickly when Uncle Jack came back from the washroom.
He asked Mr. Bungee, "How much for this carpet?"

Mr. Bungee answered,

" Two Million Dollars ! "

All the family smiles turned to sad disappointed faces.

Sad ! *Sad !* *Sad !*

Uncle Jack looked angry and said,
"Oh, that's a mean trick!
Why did you tell us that the carpet was meant for us?
You must have known that we couldn't possibly afford it."

WE SELL MAGIC CARPETS

Chapter Six

Things Change

Mr. Bungee smiled and said,
"I have a deal for you because you're my relatives."

Boing ! Boing ! Boing !

He was still bouncing up and down.
"You pay one thousand dollars now and ten dollars a month for ever
and ever. If you miss a payment, the carpet flies back to my shop."

Uncle Jack smiled and said, "It's a deal."
Then he shook Mr. Bungee's hand.
This was difficult because Mr. Bungee was still bobbing.

Uncle Jack paid Mr. Bungee from the big wad of money he kept in the
secret side pocket of his big black boots.

Hug ! Hug ! Hug !

Everyone hugged to celebrate.

Boing ! Boing ! Boing !

Mr. Bungee carried the carpet out to the car, bobbing all the way, only
stopping to tie it to the roof.

Jake, his aunt, uncle and cousins headed for home.

They were all excited. They wanted to ride the magic carpet.

As Uncle Jack drove, they all talked at the same time.

"Piff piff, boom boom, I sure am itchy," complained Jake as he scratched.

"Fuddle duddle, fuddle duddle, me too," said Uncle Jack.

Then they all scratched.

Aunt Joan screamed,
"That carpet must be full of fleas; we have to take it back!"

"Oh! No!" cried Zac.
The stiff black hairs fell down to the top of his ears.

Jake cried, "Oh! Oh! Oh, my!
Stop the car. I have get someone to scratch my back."

They were all scratching so hard Uncle Jack had to stop the car.

Everyone got out to scratch each other's backs.

Aunt Joan moaned,
"Oh, right there in the middle of my back, where I can't reach."

"Same here," said Zac.

"Me too, right in the middle between my shoulder blades," said Zoe.

"I'll just rub my back on the car," said Jake.

Itchy ! Scratch !

"Let's go!" called Uncle Jack.

Itchy ! Scratch !

Everyone continued scratching each other as they got back in the car.

Angry ! Angry ! Angry !

Uncle Jack had an angry look on his face.

He quickly and quietly drove backwards to Mr. Bungee's store.
He didn't say another word.
He didn't even scratch.

Mr. and Mrs. Bungee had stopped bouncing up and down.

They were standing on the street and seemed to be waiting for the family to return.

Uncle Jack jumped out of the car.
He was very angry and red in the face.

He started scratching vigorously as he approached Mr. Bungee.

Itchy ! Scratch !

Itchy ! Scratch !

Itchy ! Scratch !

Itchy ! Scratch !

Chapter Seven

Flea Kisses

Uncle Jack shouted, "This carpet has fleas!
You have to return my money and take it back."

"l was hoping you'd be back," said Mr. Bungee.
"You really are the ones, the only people the magic-flying-fleas can bite.
If they like you, they bite you.
It's not really a bite, it's just a little flea kiss.
lf they don't like you, the magic-flying-fleas won't stay with you and if
they don't stay with you, the Magic Carpet stops flying.
It's really the magic-flying-fleas that make the Magic Carpet fly.
They hear your thoughts and obey your commands.

Start bouncing up and down like Mrs. Bungee and me.
The magic-flying-fleas will go back to the carpet."

Boing ! Boing ! Boing !

"When you ride your carpet put some plastic on your bottom and they
won't give you flea kisses."

"Why didn't you tell us the truth in the first place?" asked Uncle Jack.

Mr. Bungee answered,
"I can only reveal the secret to people that the magic-flying-fleas bite."

Mrs. Bungee smiled and said, "I must say, it's so very nice to have you and your family as relatives.

This is the time for the magic-flying-flea dance."
She sang,
♫ *Now everyone bounce up and down.*
Turn around twice, scratch your back, and move your legs around.
Now turn and scratch your neighbors head.
Don't forget behind their ears.
That's the place fleas most like to kiss .
Their bites bring us to tears.♫

Everyone did just that and what fun it was.

People driving past honked their horns at the sight.
They must have thought it was some kind of new dance.

"Piff piff, boom boom, listen, you can hear the fleas laugh.
They sound like children's happy giggles," observed Jake.

Jake, Aunt Joan, Zoe, Zac, Uncle Jack, and Mr. and Mrs. Bungee stopped bouncing, and hugged and scratched one another.

Hug ! Hug ! Hug !

Itchy ! Scratch !

Jake could see the magic-flying-fleas and hear their

buzz z z buzz z z

buzz z z

buz z z as they jumped back into the carpet.

Zac threw his arms up in the air and said,
"I knew this was going to be a special birthday."

Uncle Jack whispered something in Jake's ear.

As they drove home, Jake thought,
This is the best day ever.
Uncle Jack told me I can be a Magic Carpet Pilot whenever I visit them.

He was happy the itch was gone.
The magic-flying-fleas,were back where they should be . . .
waiting for Jake to have his next Magic Carpet ride.

www.ingramcontent.com/pod-product-compliance
Lightning Source LLC
LaVergne TN
LVHW072108070426
835509LV00002B/68